DISNEYLAND PARIS

Discovering the Enchantment of Disneyland Paris

Ian Vaughan

Disclaimer

other people. If you would like to share this book with another person, please purchase an additional copy for each recipient. If youre reading this book and did not purchase it, or it was not purchased for your use only, then please return to your favourite book retailer and purchase your own copy. Thank you for respecting the hard work of this author.

published by: Ian Vaughan

Table of Contents

Chapter 1: Introduction to Disneyland Paris

History and background of Disneyland Paris

Disneyland Paris, originally known as Euro Disneyland, is a popular theme park and resort complex located in Marne-la-Vallee, France. It was the first Disney theme park to be built outside of the United States and was officially opened on April 12, 1992. The park covers an area of approximately 4,800 acres and is situated about 20 miles east of the city of Paris.

The idea of creating a Disney park in Europe was initiated by Michael Eisner, the CEO of The Walt Disney Company, in the 1980s. Eisner believed that a European Disney park would be a great opportunity to tap into the large tourist market in Europe and provide the Disney experience to a whole new audience.

The construction of Disneyland Paris faced various challenges, including cultural differences, financing difficulties, and concerns about preserving the French identity. The

French government provided substantial support for the project, and the Walt Disney Company formed a partnership with the French government to develop the park.

Disneyland Paris was designed as a combination of two theme parks: Disneyland Park and Walt Disney Studios Park. Disneyland Park, also known as Parc Disneyland, is the centrepiece of the resort and is inspired by the original Disneyland in California. It is divided into five themed lands: Main Street, U.S.A., Adventureland, Frontierland, Fantasyland, and Discoveryland.

Walt Disney Studios Park, on the other hand, is dedicated to the world of cinema and offers visitors a behind-the-scenes experience of the movie-making process. It features various attractions, shows, and experiences related to Disney and Pixar films.

In addition to the theme parks, Disneyland Paris also includes several resort hotels, entertainment venues, shopping areas, and dining establishments. The resort has undergone expansions and renovations over the years to enhance the guest experience and introduce new attractions.

Despite its initial challenges, Disneyland Paris has become one of the most visited tourist destinations in Europe. It has attracted millions of visitors since its opening and has contributed significantly to the local economy and tourism industry.

In recent years, Disneyland Paris has continued to evolve and introduce new attractions and experiences. It has embraced seasonal events, such as Halloween and Christmas celebrations, and has also incorporated characters and stories from popular Disney franchises, such as Star Wars and Marvel.

Disneyland Paris remains an iconic symbol of Disneys global presence and serves as a cultural bridge between American entertainment and European heritage. It continues to delight visitors of all ages with its immersive storytelling, iconic characters, and magical experiences.

Understanding the layout of the park and its different areas

Disneyland Paris is divided into two main theme parks: Disneyland Park and Walt Disney Studios Park. Each park offers a unique experience with different themed lands and attractions.

Disneyland Park:

Disneyland Park is the original park in the Disneyland Paris resort and is inspired by the original Disneyland in California. It is divided into five themed lands:

a. Main Street, U.S.A.: As guests enter the park, they step into Main Street, U.S.A., a charming street designed to resemble a small American town at the turn of the 20th century. It is lined with shops, restaurants, and Victorian-style buildings.

b. Adventureland: Adventureland is themed around exotic and adventurous locations. It features attractions such as Pirates of the

Caribbean, Indiana Jones and the Temple of Peril, and the Swiss Family Treehouse. Guests can explore tropical landscapes and encounter thrilling adventures.

c. Frontierland: Frontierland takes visitors back to the Wild West era with a frontier town atmosphere. It includes attractions such as Big Thunder Mountain, Phantom Manor (a haunted mansion), and the River Rogue Keelboats. Guests can experience the spirit of the Old West and embark on exciting adventures.

d. Fantasyland: Fantasyland is a whimsical land where classic Disney fairy tales come to life. It features iconic attractions such as Sleeping Beauty Castle, Peter Pans Flight, Its a Small World, and Dumbo the Flying Elephant. Guests can meet Disney princesses, go on enchanting rides, and immerse themselves in magical stories.

e. Discoveryland: Discoveryland is dedicated to the future and exploration. It incorporates elements of science fiction and futuristic technology. Attractions in this land include Space Mountain: Mission 2, Buzz Lightyear Laser Blast, and Star Tours: The Adventures Continue. Guests can experience space travel, encounter aliens, and embrace futuristic adventures.

Walt Disney Studios Park:
Walt Disney Studios Park is
dedicated to the world of cinema and
provides a behind-the-scenes look at
the movie-making process. It is
divided into different studio-themed
areas:

a. Front Lot: Front Lot serves as the
parks entrance and resembles a
Hollywood movie studio entrance. It
features the Studio Services building
and various shops and dining options.

b. Production Courtyard: Production
Courtyard showcases the glamour of
the movie industry. It includes
attractions such as The Twilight Zone

Tower of Terror, Studio Tram Tour: Behind the Magic, and the Studio D Theater. Guests can experience thrilling rides and learn about movie production.

c. Toy Story Playland: Toy Story Playland is inspired by the beloved Toy Story movies. It offers attractions such as RC Racer, Slinky Dog Zigzag Spin, and Toy Soldiers Parachute Drop. Guests shrink down to toy size and explore the world of toys.

d. Backlot: Backlot is an area dedicated to action and special effects. It features attractions such as Ratatouille: The Adventure, Rock n Roller Coaster starring Aerosmith, and Armageddon: Les Effets Spéciaux. Guests can experience high-speed adventures and witness spectacular special effects.

e. Toon Studio: Toon Studio celebrates the art of animation. It includes attractions such as Crushs Coaster, Cars Quatre Roues Rallye, and Flying Carpets Over Agrabah. Guests can enter the world of beloved Disney and Pixar animated characters.

Apart from the theme parks, Disneyland Paris also includes other areas such as Disney Village, a dining, shopping, and entertainment district, and several resort hotels that cater to different themes and budgets. Overall, the layout of Disneyland Paris is designed to provide a diverse range of experiences, from magical fairy tales to cinematic adventures, offering something for everyone.

Discover the magic and unique features that make Disneyland Paris a special destination

Disneyland Paris is a truly special destination that captures the hearts and imaginations of visitors from around the world. It offers a multitude of unique features and magical experiences that make it stand out among other theme parks. Lets delve into what makes Disneyland Paris so special:

European Charm and Cultural Fusion:
Disneyland Paris seamlessly blends
the enchantment of Disney with the
rich cultural heritage of Europe. The
park incorporates French architecture,
landscapes, and cuisine, creating a
unique and immersive experience.
From the ornate details of Sleeping
Beauty Castle to the charming streets
of Main Street, U.S.A., every element
reflects the European charm, making
guests feel like they have stepped into
a fairytale.

Sleeping Beauty Castle:
The iconic centrepiece of Disneyland
Park is Sleeping Beauty Castle. This
magnificent castle serves as the

symbol of the park and is inspired by various European fairy tales and castles. It features stunning architecture, intricate details, and a dragon animatronic in the dungeon. Inside the castle, visitors can explore La Galerie de la Belle au Bois Dormant, an exhibition showcasing storybook scenes from Sleeping Beauty.

Unique Attractions:
Disneyland Paris offers a blend of classic Disney attractions and unique experiences found only in this park. For example, Ratatouille: The Adventure takes guests on a 4D adventure through Gusteaus restaurant, shrinking them down to

the size of a rat. Crushs Coaster allows guests to spin and whirl through an underwater adventure with Crush from Finding Nemo. These exclusive attractions provide a fresh and exciting experience for visitors.

Seasonal Celebrations:
Disneyland Paris embraces the magic of the changing seasons with vibrant celebrations and events throughout the year. From Halloween parties with spooky decorations and themed shows to Christmas festivities featuring enchanting lights and a festive parade, each season brings its own unique charm to the park. These seasonal celebrations add an extra layer of magic and make every visit

to Disneyland Paris a special experience.

Unique Entertainment:
Disneyland Paris offers a wide range of entertainment options that captivate guests of all ages. The park hosts spectacular shows, parades, and nighttime spectaculars that showcase Disneys iconic characters and stories. The nighttime spectacular, Disney Illuminations, combines fireworks, projection mapping, and music to create a dazzling visual extravaganza that lights up Sleeping Beauty Castle.

Character Interactions:
Meeting beloved Disney characters is a highlight of any visit to Disneyland

Paris. Guests can have personal interactions and take photos with Mickey Mouse, Minnie Mouse, Disney princesses, and many more characters. The park also offers character dining experiences, where guests can enjoy a meal while characters make special appearances, creating cherished memories for children and adults alike.

Disneyland Paris Exclusive Merchandise:
The resort boasts an impressive selection of exclusive merchandise, offering unique souvenirs that cant be found elsewhere. From apparel and accessories to collectibles and limited-edition items, guests can

bring a piece of the magic home with them. The merchandise reflects the creativity and attention to detail that Disney is known for, allowing visitors to continue their Disneyland Paris experience beyond the park.

French Cuisine and Dining Experiences:
Disneyland Paris is renowned for its exceptional dining options. The resort offers a variety of restaurants, ranging from quick-service eateries to fine dining experiences. Guests can indulge in delicious French cuisine, international dishes, and themed dining experiences. From character breakfasts to romantic dinners, the dining options cater to all tastes and

add an extra touch of luxury to the Disneyland Paris experience.

Resort Hotels and Immersive Theming:
Disneyland Paris offers a range of themed resort hotels that transport guests into different worlds. From the Victorian elegance of Disneyland Hotel to the African savannah-inspired Disneys Animal Kingdom Lodge, each hotel provides unique theming and immersive experiences. Staying at one of these hotels allows guests to extend their magical experience and enjoy additional perks such as Extra Magic Hours.

Ongoing Expansion and Innovation:

Disneyland Paris continuously evolves to bring new experiences and attractions to its visitors. Over the years, the resort has undergone expansions and renovations, introducing new lands, attractions, and shows. The addition of Star Wars: Galaxys Edge and the upcoming Avengers Campus showcases Disneyland Paris commitment to keeping up with the latest trends and offering cutting-edge experiences.

Best Time to Visit Disneyland Paris
The best time to visit Disneyland Paris depends on various factors such as weather, crowd levels, and special

events. Heres an extensive guide to help you plan your visit:

Weather: The climate in Disneyland Paris can vary throughout the year. The park experiences four distinct seasons. Spring (March to May) and autumn (September to November) offer mild temperatures and fewer crowds, making them pleasant times to visit. Summers (June to August) can be warm, but the parks are busiest during this time. Winters (December to February) are colder, and some attractions may be closed for maintenance, but you can experience the parks enchanting holiday season.

Crowd Levels: Disneyland Paris attracts visitors from around the world, and crowd levels can significantly impact your experience. If you want to avoid large crowds, consider visiting during weekdays outside of school holidays. September and October, excluding school breaks, tend to have lower attendance. Additionally, weekdays in May, early June, and late August can be less crowded.

Special Events: Disneyland Paris hosts various special events throughout the year, which can enhance your visit. Here are some notable events to consider:

Disneys Halloween Festival: Usually held from late September to early November, this event features spooky decorations, themed parades, and special shows.

Disneys Enchanted Christmas: From mid-November to early January, the park is transformed into a winter wonderland, with festive decorations, special shows, and a grand Christmas parade.

Disney FanDaze: This event celebrates Disney fandom and typically takes place in early summer. It includes character meet-and-greets, exclusive shows, and unique entertainment.

Star Wars Legends: If youre a Star Wars fan, visiting during the Star Wars Legends event, typically held in early spring, can provide a unique experience with themed activities and encounters with beloved characters.

Park Hours: Check the official Disneyland Paris website or app for the parks opening hours during your planned visit. The park usually opens at 10:00 AM and closes between 6:00 PM and 12:00 AM, depending on the season and day of the week. Arriving early or staying late can give you extra time to enjoy attractions with shorter queues.

Annual Passes: If you plan to visit Disneyland Paris multiple times within a year, consider purchasing an Annual Pass. It provides various benefits such as discounts on merchandise and dining, exclusive events, and early access to certain attractions.

Plan and Book in Advance: To make the most of your visit, plan your itinerary in advance. Research the parks attractions, shows, and dining options to prioritise what you want to experience. Make dining reservations and FastPass selections (if available) to minimise wait times. Additionally, booking your tickets and accommodation well in advance can help secure better deals and availability.

Check for Refurbishments: Before your visit, check if any major attractions or areas of the park are undergoing refurbishment. This information is usually available on the official Disneyland Paris website. By being aware of any closures or renovations, you can adjust your itinerary accordingly.

Travel Requirements

When planning a trip to Disneyland Paris, its important to be aware of the travel requirements to ensure a smooth and enjoyable experience. Here are some key considerations:

Passport: Before travelling to Disneyland Paris, ensure that your passport is valid for at least six months beyond your planned departure date. This requirement is essential for entry into France. If your passport is nearing expiration, its advisable to renew it before your trip.

Visa: Depending on your nationality, you may need a visa to enter France. Citizens of many countries, including the United States, Canada, the United Kingdom, and countries within the Schengen Area, typically do not require a visa for short-term visits (usually up to 90 days). However, its essential to check the French embassy or consulate website in your country for the most up-to-date information on visa requirements.

COVID-19 Restrictions: Due to the ongoing COVID-19 pandemic, additional travel requirements and restrictions may be in place. These measures can vary depending on the current situation and government guidelines. Before your trip, check the official Disneyland Paris website and the French governments travel advisory for the latest information on COVID-19 entry requirements. This may include proof of vaccination, negative COVID-19 test results, or other health-related documentation.

Travel Insurance: Its strongly recommended to have travel insurance that covers medical emergencies, trip cancellations, and other unforeseen events. Travel insurance can provide financial protection and peace of mind in case of unexpected situations, such as illness, injury, or trip disruptions.

Flights: To reach Disneyland Paris, you can book flights to either Charles de Gaulle Airport (CDG) or Orly Airport (ORY), both located near Paris. These airports have good transportation connections to the city and Disneyland Paris. Consider factors such as flight availability, prices, and layovers when selecting your flights.

Transportation: Once you arrive in Paris, you can choose from various transportation options to reach Disneyland Paris, which is located approximately 32 kilometres (20 miles) east of the city centre. The most convenient method is by using the RER A train line. The RER A has a direct service from central Paris to the Marne-la-Vallee/Chessy station, which is right at the entrance of Disneyland Paris. Another option is to take a shuttle bus service from Paris city centre or the airports. Additionally, you can rent a car or take a taxi for more flexibility and convenience.

Accommodation: Disneyland Paris offers a range of accommodation options, including Disney hotels and nearby partner hotels. Staying at a Disney hotel provides a more immersive experience, with easy access to the parks and additional perks like Extra Magic Hours. However, these options can be more expensive. Partner hotels, located near Disneyland Paris, offer a variety of choices at different price points. Its advisable to book your accommodation in advance, especially during peak seasons, to secure your preferred choice.

Park Tickets: To access Disneyland Park and Walt Disney Studios Park, you need to purchase park tickets. Its recommended to buy your tickets online in advance to save time and avoid long queues at the park entrance. The official Disneyland Paris website provides detailed information on ticket options, prices, and any available promotions.

Currency: The official currency in France is the Euro (€). Its advisable to have some cash on hand for smaller expenses, such as food and souvenirs. While credit and debit cards are widely accepted in most places, including Disneyland Paris, its always a good idea to carry some cash for emergencies or situations where card payments may not be possible.

Language: The official language in France is French. However, English is widely spoken in tourist areas, including Disneyland Paris. Cast members at the park are usually bilingual and can assist you in English. Nevertheless, its helpful to learn a few basic French phrases, such as greetings and simple expressions, to enhance your experience and show appreciation for the local culture.

Weather and Clothing: Consider the weather conditions during your visit to Disneyland Paris and pack accordingly. The climate in Paris is generally mild, with warm summers and cold winters. Bring comfortable walking shoes, lightweight clothing for the summer months, and warmer layers for cooler seasons. Its also advisable to carry a waterproof jacket or umbrella, as rain showers are possible throughout the year.

Health and Safety: Prioritise your health and safety during your trip. Its recommended to check if you need any specific vaccinations before travelling to France. Ensure that you have any necessary medications or prescriptions with you, along with travel-sized first aid essentials.

Familiarise yourself with emergency contact numbers and the location of medical facilities near Disneyland Paris.

Local Customs and Etiquette: While visiting Disneyland Paris, be respectful of local customs and etiquette. Politeness, patience, and cultural sensitivity go a long way in creating a positive experience. Familiarise yourself with basic French customs, such as greeting with "Bonjour" (hello) and saying "Merci" (thank you). Follow park rules and guidelines, and be considerate of other visitors.

Plan and Research: To make the most of your trip to Disneyland Paris, plan and research in advance. Study the park maps, show schedules, and attractions to prioritise your must-see experiences. Make dining reservations, especially for popular restaurants, to avoid disappointment. Disneyland Paris offers a range of entertainment, parades, and special events throughout the year, so check the official website for the latest updates and schedules.

Stay Informed: Keep yourself updated with the latest travel advisories, park announcements, and any changes in travel requirements before and during your trip. Official sources such as the Disneyland Paris website, the French governments travel advisory, and your countrys embassy or consulate can provide the most accurate and up-to-date information.

By following these travel requirements and guidelines, you can ensure a smooth and enjoyable trip to Disneyland Paris.

Common Rules and Regulations

When visiting Disneyland Paris, its essential to familiarise yourself with the rules and regulations to ensure a safe and enjoyable experience for all guests. The park has specific guidelines in place to maintain a welcoming and family-friendly environment. Here are some of the main rules governing Disneyland Paris:

General Conduct:

- Respect others: Guests are expected to treat fellow visitors, cast members (Disney employees), and Disney characters with respect and courtesy.
- Proper attire: Guests are required to wear appropriate clothing at all times. Offensive or inappropriate attire, including clothing with

offensive language or imagery, is not permitted.
- No smoking: Smoking is strictly prohibited inside the park, except in designated smoking areas.
- No running: Running is discouraged to maintain a safe environment for everyone.
- Line etiquette: Guests are expected to wait patiently in line and follow the instructions of the cast members.

Safety:

- Security screening: All guests and their belongings are

subject to security screening upon entry.

- Bag checks: Bags may be subject to inspection, and large bags or backpacks may need to be stored in lockers or designated areas.
- Height and age restrictions: Some attractions have specific height or age requirements for safety reasons. Its important to follow these guidelines to ensure a safe experience.
- Prohibited items: Certain items, such as weapons, alcohol, drones, and glass containers, are not allowed inside the park.

- Accessibility: Disneyland Paris strives to be accessible to guests with disabilities. Wheelchair and stroller rentals are available, and there are designated areas for viewing parades and shows.

Photography and Filming:

- Personal use only: Photography and filming are permitted for personal use only. Commercial use, including selling or publishing images or videos, is strictly prohibited without prior authorization.

- No selfie sticks: The use of selfie sticks is not allowed on attractions or in any area where they may pose a safety hazard to other guests.

Food and Drink:

- Outside food and beverages: Guests are allowed to bring their own food and non-alcoholic beverages into the park. However, glass containers and coolers on wheels are not permitted.
- Alcohol consumption: Alcohol is available in certain areas of the park, but guests must be of legal drinking age

and follow the parks guidelines regarding alcohol consumption.

Park Operations:

- Opening hours: Disneyland Paris has specific opening and closing times. Its advisable to check the official website or park schedule for the most up-to-date information.
- FastPass system: The park offers a FastPass system that allows guests to reserve a specific time slot for popular attractions, reducing waiting times.

- Park closures and attractions maintenance: Some attractions may be temporarily closed for maintenance or refurbishment. These closures are typically scheduled in advance and can be found on the parks official website.

Its important to note that Disneyland Paris reserves the right to refuse entry or remove any guest who fails to comply with the parks rules and regulations. By following these guidelines, visitors can help create a magical and enjoyable experience for themselves and fellow guests.

Common Language Conversations

When visiting Disneyland Paris, its helpful to familiarise yourself with some common language conversations that can enhance your experience and interaction with the cast members (Disney employees) and fellow visitors. Here are some phrases and conversations that can be useful during your visit:

Greetings and Basic Phrases:

- Hello! / Hi! - Bonjour! (bohn-zhoor)
- Goodbye! - Au revoir! (oh ruh-vwah)

- Please - Sil vous plaît (seel voo pleh)
- Thank you - Merci (mehr-see)
- Youre welcome - De rien (duh ree-ehn)
- Excuse me - Excusez-moi (ex-kyoo-zay mwa)
- Sorry - Pardon (pahr-dohn)
- Yes - Oui (wee)
- No - Non (nohn)

Asking for Help and Information:

- Can you help me, please? - Pouvez-vous maider, sil vous plaît? (poovay-voo may-day, seel voo pleh)
- Where is...? - Où est...? (oo ay)

- Where are the restrooms? - Où sont les toilettes? (oo sohn lay twah-let)
- What time does the parade start? - À quelle heure commence le défilé? (ah kell uhr koh-mahns luh day-fih-lay)
- Is there a FastPass for this attraction? - Y a-t-il un FastPass pour cette attraction? (ee-yah-teel un FastPass poor set at-trak-see-yon)

Ordering Food and Beverages:

- I would like... - Je voudrais... (zhuh voo-dray)

- A bottle of water, please - Une bouteille deau, sil vous plaît (oon boot-ay doh, seel voo pleh)
- Can I have a menu, please? - Puis-je avoir un menu, sil vous plaît? (pwee-zhuh ah-vwar un meh-nyoo, seel voo pleh)
- How much does it cost? - Combien ça coûte? (kohm-byen sah koot)
- Is there a vegetarian option? - Y a-t-il une option végétarienne? (ee-yah-teel oon op-see-yon vey-zhay-tah-ree-ehn)

Attraction and Ride Conversations:

- How long is the wait time for this attraction? - Combien de temps dattente pour cette attraction? (kohm-byen duh tahnt poor set at-trak-see-yon)
- Are there any height or age restrictions? - Y a-t-il des restrictions de taille ou dâge? (ee-yah-teel day rees-trik-syons duh tah-yuh oo dahzh)
- Is this ride suitable for young children? - Cette attraction convient-elle aux jeunes enfants? (set at-trak-see-yon kohn-vee-ehn-tell oh zhuhnuh-zhan-fahn)
- How many people can ride at once? - Combien de personnes

peuvent monter à la fois?
(kohm-byen duh pair-sohn
puh-vohn mohn-tay ah lah
fwah)

Interacting with Characters:

- May I have a photo with you?
  - Puis-je prendre une photo
  avec vous? (pwee-zhuh pruhn-
  druhn oon foh-toh ah-vehk
  voo)
- Youre my favorite character! -
  Vous êtes mon personnage
  préféré! (voo zet mohn pair-
  soh-nazh pray-fay-ray)
- Can you sign my autograph
  book? - Pouvez-vous signer
  mon livre dautographes?

(poovay-voo seeneh mohn
leev doh-toh-graf)

Remember, many cast members and
visitors at Disneyland Paris speak
English, so dont hesitate to ask for
assistance if needed. Being polite,
patient, and respectful will go a long
way in creating a positive experience
for everyone.

Chapter 2: Exploring Disneyland Park

Detailed descriptions of the different lands within Disneyland Park

Disneyland Paris Park is divided into several lands, each with its own distinct theming and attractions. Lets explore detailed descriptions of these lands within Disneyland Paris Park.

Main Street, U.S.A.:
As you enter Disneyland Paris Park, you are transported to Main Street, U.S.A., a charming and bustling street

that captures the essence of early 20th-century America. Adorned with Victorian-style architecture, gas lamps, and a quaint horse-drawn streetcar, this land immerses you in a nostalgic atmosphere. Stroll down the street, explore unique shops, enjoy delectable treats, and witness lively parades and entertainment.

Frontierland:
Step into the wild and adventurous Frontierland, which pays homage to the American Old West. This land is filled with rustic buildings, saloons, and a mighty river. Board the iconic steam-powered riverboat, the Mark Twain Riverboat, and set sail on the Rivers of the Far West. Brave the

thrilling Big Thunder Mountain roller coaster, which takes you on a high-speed journey through an abandoned mining town. Frontierland also features the Pocahontas Indian Village, where you can explore Native American culture and traditions.

Adventureland:
Embark on exciting expeditions in Adventureland, a land inspired by exploration and discovery. Wander through lush tropical foliage and encounter mysterious ruins as you explore the dense jungles. Sail away on the Pirates of the Caribbean attraction, where youll encounter swashbuckling pirates and a grand

pirate battle. Experience the exhilarating Indiana Jones and the Temple of Peril roller coaster or take a leisurely boat ride on Le Passage Enchanté dAladdin, a charming journey through the story of Aladdin.

Fantasyland:
Fantasyland is a magical land where fairy tales come to life. Enter through the enchanting Sleeping Beauty Castle and immerse yourself in a world of wonder and fantasy. Experience classic Disney tales on attractions such as Peter Pans Flight, where you soar above London and Neverland, and Its a Small World, a gentle boat ride showcasing the diverse cultures of the world. Visit

Alices Curious Labyrinth and explore the whimsical world of Wonderland. Meet beloved Disney characters and witness captivating live shows in this enchanting land.

Discoveryland:
Step into the future with Discoveryland, a land dedicated to imagination, innovation, and exploration. This futuristic land showcases a blend of Jules Verne-inspired steampunk aesthetics and retro-futuristic designs. Embark on a thrilling space journey on Space Mountain: Mission 2, a high-speed roller coaster that propels you through the darkness of outer space. Discover the mysteries of the Nautilus

submarine in Les Mystères du Nautilus, and take a spin on the Orbitron, a retro-futuristic flying saucer attraction.

Walt Disney Studios Park:
Adjacent to Disneyland Paris Park is Walt Disney Studios Park, a separate park that showcases the magic of movies, animation, and television. This park is divided into four studio-themed lots: Front Lot, Production Courtyard, Toy Story Playland, and Backlot. Explore the world of cinema, experience thrilling attractions, and immerse yourself in the behind-the-scenes magic of moviemaking.

Each land within Disneyland Paris Park offers a unique and immersive experience, with its own theming, attractions, and atmosphere. From the nostalgia of Main Street, U.S.A. to the thrilling adventures of Adventureland, and from the magical fairy tales of Fantasyland to the futuristic wonders of Discoveryland, Disneyland Paris Park promises unforgettable memories and enchantment for visitors of all ages.

Highlights of the must-see attractions, shows, and parades

Disneyland Paris is renowned for its captivating attractions, spectacular shows, and dazzling parades. Here are some of the must-see highlights that make the park a truly magical experience:

Attractions:

Pirates of the Caribbean: Embark on a thrilling boat ride through pirate-infested waters. This classic attraction takes you on a swashbuckling adventure, featuring animatronic pirates, treasure caves, and a captivating pirate battle.

Space Mountain: Mission 2: Brace yourself for a thrilling journey to the stars on this high-speed roller coaster. Blast off into space, experience intense twists and turns, and immerse yourself in the excitement of intergalactic travel.

Big Thunder Mountain: This exhilarating roller coaster takes you on a runaway mine train through the heart of a haunted mountain. Hold on tight as you zoom through thrilling drops, sharp turns, and breathtaking scenery.

Ratatouille: The Adventure: Shrink down to the size of a rat and join Remy from the Disney-Pixar film "Ratatouille" on a culinary adventure. Board your rat-shaped vehicle and scurry through Gusteaus restaurant, experiencing 4D effects and delightful surprises.

Its a Small World: This iconic boat ride is a celebration of global unity and diversity. Cruise through scenes representing different cultures and regions, accompanied by the unforgettable "Its a Small World" song.

Shows and Entertainment:

Disney Illuminations: This nighttime extravaganza is a mesmerising display of lights, projections, fireworks, and music. Watch as Sleeping Beauty Castle comes to life, with beloved Disney characters and iconic scenes from Disney films.

Mickey and the Magician: Immerse yourself in a spellbinding show where Mickey Mouse becomes a master magician. Witness stunning illusions, captivating storytelling, and appearances by beloved Disney characters.

The Lion King: Rhythms of the Pride Lands: Experience the vibrant and energetic stage show inspired by Disneys "The Lion King." Sing along to beloved songs, marvel at the incredible acrobatics, and be swept away by the African savannah.

Disney Stars on Parade: Join Mickey Mouse and his friends as they lead a dazzling parade through the streets of

Disneyland Paris. Marvel at the elaborate floats, vibrant costumes, and beloved Disney characters waving to the crowd.

Parades and Street Entertainment:

Main Street, U.S.A. Parade: This classic parade brings the charm of Main Street, U.S.A. to life with lively music, colourful floats, and beloved Disney characters. Get swept up in the excitement as the parade passes by.

Frozen Celebration: Immerse yourself in the enchanting world of "Frozen" with a lively parade featuring Anna, Elsa, Olaf, and other beloved characters. Enjoy the catchy tunes, elaborate costumes, and magical atmosphere.

The Starlit Princess Waltz: Witness a magical gathering of Disney princesses as they grace the royal stage with elegance and grace. Be captivated by their enchanting performances and the beauty of their iconic gowns.

Insider tips on optimising your experience in each area of the park

To optimise your experience in each area of Disneyland Paris, here are some insider tips that can help you make the most of your visit:

Main Street, U.S.A.:

- Arrive early: Main Street, U.S.A. tends to be less crowded in the morning, so arriving at park opening can give you a chance to explore shops and attractions with shorter wait times.
- Use the side streets: Main Street has several side streets that connect to other lands. Utilise these paths to navigate the park efficiently and avoid the main crowds.

Frontierland:

- FastPass for Big Thunder Mountain: Big Thunder Mountain is a popular attraction, so make use of the FastPass system to skip the line. Obtain your FastPass early in the day to secure a designated return time.
- Catch the shows during parade times: Since Frontierland is along the parade route, consider watching shows like "The Chaparral Theater Presents The Lion King: Rhythms of the Pride Lands" during parade hours to avoid larger crowds.

Adventureland:

- Single Rider for Indiana Jones
  and the Temple of Peril: If
  you dont mind riding alone,
  take advantage of the Single
  Rider line to experience this
  thrilling attraction with a
  shorter wait time.
- Visit Pirates of the Caribbean
  early or late: Pirates of the
  Caribbean tends to have
  shorter wait times during the
  first and last hours of park
  operation, so plan your visit
  accordingly.

Fantasyland:

- Make character meet-and-greets a priority: Fantasyland is known for its character encounters. Check the schedule for meet-and-greet locations and times to meet your favourite Disney characters.
- Utilise FastPass for popular attractions: Attractions like Peter Pans Flight and Its a Small World can have long queues. Get a FastPass to minimise wait times and maximise your experience.

Discoveryland:

- Early morning for Buzz Lightyear Laser Blast: Buzz Lightyear Laser Blast is a popular attraction. Ride it early in the morning to avoid long lines.
- Plan for Hyperspace Mountain: Hyperspace Mountain, a Star Wars-themed version of Space Mountain, can have long wait times. Consider riding it later in the day or utilising the FastPass system.

Walt Disney Studios Park:

- Use Extra Magic Hours: If youre staying at a Disney

hotel, take advantage of Extra Magic Hours to access select attractions before the park opens to the public.

- Prioritise popular attractions early: Head to popular attractions like Ratatouille: The Adventure and Crushs Coaster early in the day to experience them with shorter wait times.

General Tips:

- Download the official Disneyland Paris app: The app provides real-time information on wait times, show schedules, and interactive maps to help you plan your day efficiently.

- Take advantage of FastPass: Use the FastPass system to reserve a specific time slot for popular attractions, reducing your waiting time.
- Plan your dining in advance: Make restaurant reservations in advance, especially for popular dining locations, to secure a table at your preferred time.
- Stay hydrated and bring snacks: Disneyland Paris allows outside food and drinks, so bring water bottles and snacks to keep you

refreshed and energised
throughout the day.

By following these insider tips, you
can optimise your experience in each
area of Disneyland Paris and make
the most of your visit, ensuring a
memorable and enjoyable time in the
park.

Chapter 3: Adventures in Walt Disney Studios Park

Overview of the unique experiences offered in Walt Disney Studios Park

Walt Disney Studios Park offers a range of unique experiences that cater to the imagination and entertainment of visitors. Lets explore some of the highlights and distinctive attractions you can enjoy in this magical theme park.

Ratatouille: The Adventure: Step into the world of the animated film "Ratatouille" and shrink down to the size of a rat. This 4D dark ride takes you on a thrilling adventure through Gusteaus restaurant in a rat-shaped vehicle, offering a unique perspective as you scurry through the kitchen and dodge oversized culinary obstacles.

Crushs Coaster: Join Crush, the sea turtle from "Finding Nemo," on a swirling underwater adventure. This spinning roller coaster takes you through the East Australian Current, providing an exhilarating experience with unexpected twists and turns.

Toy Story Playland: Enter Andys backyard and become one of Andys toys in this immersive land inspired by the "Toy Story" movies. Experience attractions like RC Racer, where you ride a remote-controlled car, and Slinky Dog Zigzag Spin, a family-friendly coaster that takes you on a spin with Slinky Dog.

The Twilight Zone Tower of Terror: This spine-tingling attraction is a must-visit for thrill-seekers. Enter the mysterious Hollywood Tower Hotel and board an elevator that takes an eerie journey through the Twilight Zone. Experience heart-pounding drops and supernatural surprises.

Mickey and the Magician: Prepare to be enchanted by this live show featuring Mickey Mouse. Witness the magic as Mickey, alongside iconic Disney characters, brings beloved fairy tales to life through stunning illusions, music, and theatrical performances.

Cars Quatre Roues Rallye: Inspired by the "Cars" movies, this ride lets you join Lightning McQueen and Mater in a fun-filled race around Radiator Springs. Hop into one of the carriages and enjoy the spinning and tilting motions as you navigate the track.

Studio Tram Tour: Behind the Magic: Embark on a backstage adventure and discover the secrets of movie-making. This guided tour takes you through real film sets, showcases special effects, and offers a glimpse into the art of creating movie magic.

Moteurs... Action! Stunt Show Spectacular: Get ready for high-octane action as stunt performers demonstrate thrilling vehicle stunts, explosions, and daring manoeuvres. This live show provides an exciting behind-the-scenes look at how action sequences are created for the movies.

Art of Disney Animation: Step into the world of Disney animation and learn about the artistry and creativity that goes into bringing beloved characters to life. Experience interactive exhibits, watch short films, and even get a chance to learn how to draw a Disney character.

Animagique: Join Mickey Mouse on a whimsical musical adventure celebrating the magic of animation. This colourful and enchanting show combines live-action, music, and Disney characters to create a captivating experience for all ages

Chapter 4: Dining and Entertainment

Recommendations for dining options within Disneyland Paris, from quick-service to fine dining

When it comes to dining options within Disneyland Paris, there is a wide range of choices available, catering to various tastes and preferences. From quick-service restaurants to fine dining establishments, the park offers a diverse selection of culinary experiences. Whether youre in the mood for a quick bite or a leisurely meal, Disneyland Paris has something to satisfy every appetite.

Quick-Service Restaurants: Quick-service restaurants are perfect for those looking for a convenient and efficient dining experience, allowing you to maximise your time in the park. Here are some top recommendations:
a. Caseys Corner: Located on Main Street, U.S.A., this American-style eatery is famous for its hot dogs and corn dog nuggets. The nostalgic baseball theme and live piano music add to the ambiance.

b. Hakuna Matata: Situated in Adventureland, this restaurant offers a selection of African and Indian-inspired dishes. Try their tasty wraps, salads, and grilled specialties, perfect for a quick and flavorful meal.
c. Fuente del Oro Restaurante: Found in Frontierland, this Mexican restaurant serves up delicious Tex-Mex cuisine. From burritos to fajitas, youll find a variety of options to satisfy your hunger.

Table-Service Restaurants:
Table-service restaurants provide a more relaxed dining experience, allowing you to sit back, enjoy your meal, and immerse yourself in the

magical atmosphere of Disneyland Paris. Here are a few notable choices: a. Auberge de Cendrillon: Located in Fantasyland, this enchanting restaurant offers a fairy-tale dining experience. Enjoy French cuisine while being surrounded by the story of Cinderella. This is an excellent choice for families and fans of classic Disney princesses.
b. Blue Lagoon Restaurant: Situated within Pirates of the Caribbean attraction in Adventureland, this unique restaurant offers a tropical setting with a view of the pirate-infested waters. Indulge in a range of seafood dishes and international cuisine as you soak in the atmosphere.

c. Walts - An American Restaurant: Found on Main Street, U.S.A., this elegant establishment pays tribute to the visionary behind Disneyland, Walt Disney himself. Enjoy a refined dining experience while admiring the park from above. The menu features a mix of French and American cuisine, with options for every palate.

Fine Dining Restaurants:
For a truly upscale dining experience, Disneyland Paris boasts a selection of fine dining establishments that combine exquisite cuisine with impeccable service. Here are a couple of recommendations:
a. Auberge du Pays de France: Situated in the heart of Disneyland

Park, this elegant restaurant offers refined French cuisine in a sophisticated setting. Indulge in gourmet dishes and savour the flavours of France prepared with meticulous attention to detail.

b. California Grill: Located in the Disneyland Hotel, this upscale restaurant offers breathtaking views of the parks fireworks and Sleeping Beauty Castle. The menu features a fusion of California and French cuisine, and the extensive wine list complements the dining experience perfectly.

Remember to make advanced reservations for table-service and fine dining restaurants to secure your preferred dining times, especially during peak seasons. Disneyland Paris offers various meal plans and packages, allowing you to enhance your dining experience and make the most of your visit.

Please note that restaurant availability and menus may change over time, so its always a good idea to check the official Disneyland Paris website or consult with guest services for the most up-to-date information on dining options and reservations.

Enjoy your culinary adventure at Disneyland Paris!

Insight into character dining experiences and themed restaurants

Character dining experiences and themed restaurants add an extra touch of magic to dining at Disneyland Paris. These unique dining options allow guests to interact with beloved Disney characters while enjoying a delicious meal. Lets delve into the world of character dining experiences and themed restaurants at Disneyland Paris.

Character Dining Experiences: Character dining experiences are a fantastic way to meet and greet Disney characters while indulging in a delightful meal. Here are a few noteworthy options:

a. Auberge de Cendrillon: This enchanting restaurant in Fantasyland offers a character dining experience fit for royalty. Meet Disney princesses such as Cinderella, Belle, and Snow White as you enjoy a delectable meal. This is an excellent choice for families and fans of classic Disney princesses.

b. Inventions: Located in the Disneyland Hotel, Inventions offers a delightful buffet meal with a wide range of dishes inspired by international cuisine. This restaurant hosts various Disney characters, including Mickey Mouse, Minnie Mouse, and their friends, making it a memorable experience for guests of all ages.

c. Plaza Gardens Restaurant: Situated on Main Street, U.S.A., this buffet restaurant is known for its international cuisine and lively atmosphere. Meet classic Disney characters like Mickey Mouse, Pluto, and friends as you enjoy your meal. Its a popular choice for families looking to have a fun-filled dining experience.

Themed Restaurants:
Disneyland Paris is renowned for its immersive theming, and themed restaurants play a significant role in enhancing the overall dining experience. Here are a few themed

restaurants that offer an immersive atmosphere:

a. Captain Jacks - Restaurant des Pirates: Located in Adventureland, this restaurant is set within the Pirates of the Caribbean attraction. Enjoy a meal in a pirate-themed setting, surrounded by treasures, cannons, and pirate decor. The ambiance perfectly complements the adventurous spirit of the attraction.

b. Bistrot Chez Rémy: Situated in Walt Disney Studios Park, this Ratatouille-themed restaurant takes guests into the world of the lovable rat chef, Rémy. The restaurant recreates the ambiance of Gusteaus restaurant from the movie, with oversized props and theming that makes you feel like youve shrunk down to rat size. The French-inspired menu offers a range of delectable dishes.

c. Hakuna Matata: Found in Adventureland, this Lion King-themed restaurant immerses guests in the African savannah. The vibrant decor, inspired by the film, sets the stage for a lively dining experience. Indulge in African and Indian-inspired cuisine, including wraps, salads, and grilled specialties.

Its important to note that character dining experiences and themed restaurants are popular, and advanced reservations are highly recommended. Availability may vary, so its advisable to check the Disneyland Paris website or consult with guest services for the latest information and to secure your preferred dining times.

These dining experiences provide an excellent opportunity to capture memorable photos with your favourite Disney characters and immerse yourself in the magic of Disneyland Paris. Whether youre dining with princesses or enjoying a meal in a themed environment, character dining experiences and themed restaurants are sure to create unforgettable moments during your visit.

An overview of the various entertainment offerings, including nighttime shows and special events

Disneyland Paris offers a wide array of entertainment offerings, including nighttime shows and special events, designed to captivate and delight guests of all ages. From dazzling fireworks displays to immersive parades and seasonal celebrations, there is always something magical happening at Disneyland Paris.

Nighttime Shows:
a. Disney Illuminations: This breathtaking nighttime spectacular takes place in front of Sleeping Beauty Castle in Disneyland Park.

Featuring projection mapping, fireworks, lasers, and beloved Disney characters, Disney Illuminations combines music and storytelling to create a mesmerising experience.

b. Disney Dreams! of Christmas: During the holiday season, Disney Dreams! Christmas takes centre stage with a festive twist. This show incorporates holiday-themed projections, fireworks, and Christmas songs, spreading holiday cheer throughout the park.

c. Disney Stars on Parade: This vibrant parade showcases Disney characters, elaborate floats, and catchy music as they make their way through Disneyland Park. Prepare to be enthralled by the stunning costumes and lively performances during this daytime parade.

Special Events:
a. Mickeys Halloween Party: During the Halloween season, Disneyland Paris hosts Mickeys Halloween Party, a special event filled with spooky surprises. Guests can enjoy themed parades, meet-and-greets with Disney villains, and even dress up in costumes to join the fun.
b. Disneys Enchanted Christmas: This festive celebration takes place during the holiday season, transforming the park into a winter wonderland. Guests can experience magical parades, meet Santa Claus, and enjoy themed shows

and decorations throughout both parks.

c. The Festival of Pirates and Princesses: This interactive and immersive event invites guests to choose between Team Pirates or Team Princesses and participate in a lively celebration. Colourful processions, energetic performances, and meet-and-greets with Disney characters make this event a highlight for many visitors.

Seasonal Celebrations:
a. Disneys Halloween Festival: From September to October, Disneyland Paris embraces the Halloween spirit with spooky decorations, special shows, and character meet-and-greets.

Guests can also enjoy exclusive Halloween-themed attractions and a nighttime Halloween parade.

b. Disneys Magical Fireworks and Bonfire: On selected evenings in November, Disneyland Paris hosts a magical fireworks display and bonfire. This enchanting spectacle is accompanied by music and stunning visual effects, creating a memorable experience for all.

c. Disneys Enchanted Advent Calendar: From December 1st to 24th, guests can witness the lighting of a giant advent calendar in front of Sleeping Beauty Castle. Each day, a new window is opened, revealing surprises and enchantment for the holiday season.

Its important to note that entertainment offerings may vary throughout the year, and its advisable to check the official Disneyland Paris website or consult with guest services for the most up-to-date information on nighttime shows, special events, and seasonal celebrations.

These entertainment offerings contribute to the overall enchantment and excitement of a visit to Disneyland Paris. They create unforgettable moments and bring Disney stories to life, ensuring that every guests experience is truly magical.

Chapter 5: Shopping and Souvenirs

A guide to the diverse shopping opportunities available throughout the park

Disneyland Paris is not just a theme park, but also a shoppers paradise. From exclusive merchandise to unique souvenirs, the park offers a diverse range of shopping opportunities that cater to every taste and interest. Whether youre looking for classic Disney memorabilia, high-end fashion, or specialty items,

Disneyland Paris has it all. In this chapter, we will explore the various shopping areas within the park and highlight some of the must-visit stores and boutiques.

Main Street, U.S.A.:

As you enter Disneyland Paris, Main Street, U.S.A. welcomes you with its charming, nostalgic ambiance. This iconic street is lined with an array of shops and boutiques that capture the spirit of turn-of-the-century America. Main Street, U.S.A. is the perfect place to start your shopping adventure. Here, you will find stores like Emporium, where you can browse through a vast selection of

Disney-themed clothing, accessories, and collectibles. If youre a fan of fine art, stop by the Disney Gallery to admire and purchase beautiful Disney-inspired artwork.

Fantasyland:

Fantasyland is a magical land filled with enchanting attractions, but it also offers some delightful shopping experiences. At La Chaumière des Sept Nains, you can find an assortment of Snow White-themed merchandise, from plush toys to clothing. For those who love princesses, the Bibbidi Bobbidi Boutique is a must-visit. This charming boutique offers princess makeovers, complete with costumes and accessories. You can also find princess-inspired clothing, tiaras, and other royal treasures.

Adventureland:

Adventureland takes you on exciting journeys to exotic lands, and it also provides opportunities for unique shopping experiences. At the Bazaar, youll discover a treasure trove of Middle Eastern-inspired merchandise, including clothing, jewellery, and home decor. This is the perfect place to find that Aladdin-themed souvenir youve been dreaming of. Dont forget to visit Les Légendes dAladin, a shop dedicated to the beloved Disney movie, where you can find everything from plush toys to clothing.

Frontierland:

Frontierland takes you back to the Wild West, and its shops reflect this adventurous spirit. At Thunder Mesa Mercantile Building, youll find a variety of Western-themed merchandise, including cowboy hats, apparel, and accessories. If youre a fan of Toy Story, make sure to visit the Cowboy Cookout Boutique, where you can find exclusive Toy Story-themed items. From Woody and Buzz Lightyear plush toys to clothing featuring your favourite characters, this store is a must-visit for any Toy Story enthusiast.

Discoveryland:

In Discoveryland, the futuristic-themed shops offer a unique shopping experience. At Constellations, you can explore a wide range of space-themed merchandise, including clothing, toys, and accessories. If youre a Star Wars fan, dont miss Star Traders, a store dedicated to the iconic franchise. Here, you can find everything from lightsabers and action figures to clothing inspired by the galaxy far, far away.

Val dEurope Shopping Center:

Adjacent to Disneyland Paris is the Val dEurope Shopping Center, which offers even more shopping opportunities. This expansive mall features over 190 stores, including high-end fashion brands, electronics stores, and beauty boutiques. If youre looking for a break from the Disney-themed merchandise, this is the perfect place to indulge in some retail therapy.

Tips for Shopping at Disneyland Paris:

Take note of store hours: Different stores may have varying opening and closing times, so make sure to check the schedule to plan your shopping accordingly.

Consider package delivery services: If youre concerned about carrying your purchases around the park, Disneyland Paris offers a package delivery service. You can have your items sent to the entrance or your Disney hotel, allowing you to continue enjoying the park without the burden of bags.

Look out for limited-edition items: Disneyland Paris often releases exclusive and limited-edition merchandise. Keep an eye out for these special items, as they make for unique and highly sought-after souvenirs.

Compare prices: While the merchandise at Disneyland Paris is magical, its always a good idea to compare prices and check for any discounts or promotions. Sometimes, similar items can be found at different locations within the park, so exploring different shops may lead to better deals.

Enjoy the shopping experience: Shopping at Disneyland Paris is not just about buying souvenirs; its an immersive experience. Take the time to appreciate the themed environments, interact with Cast

Members, and soak in the magical atmosphere as you shop.

Remember, shopping opportunities at Disneyland Paris are not limited to the park itself. The Disney Village, located just outside the park, also offers a variety of shops, restaurants, and entertainment options for visitors to explore.

So, whether youre a dedicated Disney fan or simply looking for unique and memorable souvenirs, Disneyland Paris provides a shopping experience that is sure to delight visitors of all ages. Enjoy exploring the diverse shopping opportunities throughout the park and create magical memories that will last a lifetime.

Information on where to find exclusive merchandise and souvenirs

When visiting a place as iconic and magical as Disneyland Paris, its only natural to want to bring home exclusive merchandise and souvenirs to commemorate your experience. Thankfully, Disneyland Paris offers a variety of locations where you can find unique and sought-after items that you wont find anywhere else. In this guide, we will explore some of the best spots within the park where you can discover exclusive merchandise and souvenirs.

La Chaumière des Sept Nains in
Fantasyland:
If youre a fan of Snow White and the
Seven Dwarfs, La Chaumière des
Sept Nains in Fantasyland is the place
to be. This charming shop is
dedicated to Snow White and offers
an array of exclusive merchandise
related to the classic fairy tale. From
plush toys and clothing to home decor
and collectibles, youll find everything
you need to bring the magic of Snow
White home with you.

Les Légendes dAladdin in
Adventureland:
Step into the world of Aladdin at Les
Légendes dAladin, a store dedicated

to the popular Disney movie. Here, youll find an extensive collection of Aladdin-themed merchandise, including clothing, accessories, toys, and more. From Jasmine-inspired costumes to Aladdin-themed home decor, this store offers exclusive items that will delight any Aladdin fan.

Star Traders in Discoveryland: Star Traders, located in Discoveryland, is a haven for Star Wars enthusiasts. This expansive store is filled with exclusive Star Wars merchandise, including lightsabers, action figures, clothing, and accessories. Whether youre looking for a collectible item or a unique Star Wars-themed gift, Star Traders has you covered. You can also find merchandise related to other popular franchises like Marvel and Indiana Jones in this store.

Val dEurope Shopping Center: Adjacent to Disneyland Paris is the Val dEurope Shopping Center, which houses a variety of stores offering exclusive merchandise and souvenirs. From the World of Disney store to boutique shops dedicated to fashion and accessories, youll find an extensive selection of Disney-themed items. Additionally, Val dEurope Shopping Center features several stores that carry high-end designer brands, luxury goods, and beauty products, providing a unique shopping experience outside the park.

Tips for Finding Exclusive Merchandise and Souvenirs:

Explore specialty shops: Keep an eye out for shops dedicated to specific characters, movies, or themes within each land of the park. These specialty shops often offer exclusive merchandise related to their respective themes.

Limited-edition releases: Disneyland Paris frequently releases limited-edition merchandise, such as pins, plush toys, and apparel. Stay updated with park announcements and events to ensure you dont miss out on these collectible items.

Visit during special occasions: Disneyland Paris often celebrates special occasions and holidays with exclusive merchandise. Christmas, Halloween, and other seasonal events offer unique souvenirs that capture the spirit of the festivities.

Check with Cast Members: The friendly Cast Members working in the stores are knowledgeable about the merchandise and can guide you to exclusive items. Dont hesitate to ask them for recommendations or inquire about any special releases.

Plan your budget: Exclusive merchandise can sometimes be pricier than regular items. Consider setting a budget beforehand, so you can prioritise the items that are most meaningful to you.

Remember, the availability of exclusive merchandise and souvenirs may vary, and some items may have limited stock. Its always a good idea to visit the stores early during your visit to ensure you have the best selection. Enjoy the hunt for exclusive treasures and bring home magical memories from your Disneyland Paris adventure.

Tips for making the most of your shopping experience while staying within your budget

Shopping at Disneyland Paris can be an exciting and magical experience, but its important to keep your budget in mind to ensure a satisfying and financially responsible trip. Here are some tips to help you make the most of your shopping experience while staying within your budget:

Set a budget: Before you embark on your shopping adventure, establish a realistic budget. Determine how much youre willing to spend on souvenirs, merchandise, and other items. Having a budget in place will help you prioritise your purchases and prevent overspending.

Research prices and compare: Take the time to research prices for the items youre interested in. You can browse online Disney stores or check out the official Disneyland Paris website to get an idea of the costs. By comparing prices, you can identify where you may find the best deals and make informed decisions while shopping in the park.

Make a shopping list: Create a list of the items you truly want to purchase during your visit. This will help you stay focused and avoid impulse buys. Prioritise the items that hold the most significance for you, whether they are exclusive merchandise or meaningful souvenirs. By having a clear list, you can make intentional purchases and resist unnecessary temptations.

Consider package delivery: Carrying around multiple bags can be cumbersome and hinder your enjoyment of the park. Disneyland Paris offers a package delivery service, allowing you to have your purchases sent to the parks entrance or your Disney hotel. Take advantage of this service to lighten your load and make your shopping experience more comfortable.

Look for deals and promotions: Keep an eye out for special deals, discounts, or promotions happening within the park. Disneyland Paris occasionally offers limited-time offers or bundled packages that can help you save money on your purchases. Check the parks website, social media channels, or inquire with Cast Members to stay updated on any ongoing promotions.

Explore different shopping areas: While its tempting to shop at the first store you encounter, take the time to explore different shopping areas throughout the park. Each land offers its own unique selection of merchandise. By exploring multiple locations, you may discover a wider variety of items and potentially find better prices or exclusive offerings.

Avoid peak times: Shopping during peak hours can lead to crowded stores and long lines, which can be overwhelming and time-consuming. Try to plan your shopping excursions during less busy times, such as early mornings or during parades or shows when many guests are occupied elsewhere. This way, you can shop more comfortably and efficiently.

Think beyond the park: Consider expanding your shopping options beyond Disneyland Paris itself. The Val dEurope Shopping Center, located adjacent to the park, offers a wide range of stores and brands, including some that may be more budget-friendly. Take a break from the park and explore this shopping centre for additional options.

Seek out free experiences: Disneyland Paris offers many free experiences that can be equally memorable as purchasing merchandise. Enjoy the parades, fireworks, character interactions, and shows that are included with your park admission. Focusing on these experiences can reduce the temptation to spend on unnecessary items.

Consider non-physical souvenirs: Not all souvenirs need to be physical items. Consider investing in experiences or memories rather than material possessions. Opt for character dining experiences, behind-the-scenes tours, or unique activities that will create lasting memories without adding to your physical belongings.

Remember, the most important aspect of your Disneyland Paris experience is the magic and joy youll create, not the number of items you bring home. By setting a budget, planning ahead, and making thoughtful choices, you can have a fulfilling shopping experience while staying within your financial means. Enjoy your time at Disneyland Paris and treasure the memories you make!

Chapter 6: Disneyland Paris with Kids

Advice for travelling to Disneyland Paris with children of different ages

Travelling to Disneyland Paris with children of different ages can be a magical and memorable experience for the whole family. However, its important to plan ahead and consider the specific needs and interests of each child to ensure a smooth and enjoyable trip. Whether you have toddlers, young children, or teenagers, here is some advice to make the most of your visit to the Happiest Place on Earth.

Toddlers (Ages 1-3):

- Be prepared: Pack essential items such as diapers, wipes, extra clothes, and snacks to keep your toddler comfortable throughout the day.
- Stroller rental: Consider renting a stroller or bringing your own to navigate the park easily and give your little one a place to rest.
- Baby care centres: Disneyland Paris has baby care centres equipped with changing

tables, nursing rooms, and feeding areas. Utilise these facilities for your toddlers needs.

- Character interactions: Toddlers often enjoy meeting their favourite Disney characters. Check the park schedule for character meet-and-greets and plan your day accordingly.

Young Children (Ages 4-8):

- Height restrictions: Check the height requirements for various attractions to ensure your child meets them. This will help you plan which rides and experiences are suitable for them.

- Pace yourself: Young children may tire quickly, so take breaks throughout the day. Find shaded areas or indoor attractions to rest and recharge.
- Character dining: Consider booking character dining experiences where your child can meet beloved characters while enjoying a meal.
- Parades and shows: The parades and shows in Disneyland Paris are captivating for young children. Check the schedule in advance and find a good

spot early to secure a good view.

Pre-teens (Ages 9-12):

- Get FastPasses: Utilise the FastPass system to minimise wait times for popular attractions. Arrive early and prioritise the rides your pre-teen is most excited about.
- Interactive experiences: Disneyland Paris offers interactive experiences like the Ratatouille Adventure and Buzz Lightyear Laser Blast. Encourage your pre-teen to engage in these immersive activities.

- Disney Village: Explore Disney Village, an entertainment district adjacent to the parks, where your pre-teen can enjoy shopping, dining, and live entertainment.
- Thrill rides: Older pre-teens might be eager to experience the more thrilling rides like Space Mountain or Indiana Jones and the Temple of Peril. Make sure they meet the height and age requirements for these attractions.

Teenagers:

- Plan together: Involve your teenagers in the trip planning process. Let them have a say in selecting attractions, dining options, and shows they are interested in.

- Photo opportunities: Encourage your teenagers to capture memories by taking photos with iconic landmarks or with their favourite characters.
- Shopping: Disneyland Paris has a variety of shops offering merchandise and souvenirs. Allocate some time for your teenagers to browse and shop for their favourite Disney-themed items.
- Nighttime spectaculars: The nighttime shows and

fireworks are not to be missed. Find a good viewing spot and enjoy the magical displays with your teenagers.

General Tips:

1. Prioritise must-do attractions: With limited time, its essential to prioritise the attractions and experiences your children are most excited about.
2. Dining reservations: Book dining reservations in advance, especially for character dining or popular restaurants. This will save you time and ensure you get the dining experiences you desire.

3. Stay hydrated: Keep your children hydrated throughout the day by carrying refillable water bottles and taking advantage of water fountains or free cups of water available at food locations.

4. Plan for breaks: Take breaks throughout the day to rest, have snacks, and recharge. Its important to pace yourselves and avoid exhaustion.

5. Stay flexible: While its good to have a plan, be open to adjustments and changes based on your childrens preferences and energy levels.

Remember, Disneyland Paris offers a wide range of attractions and experiences for children of all ages. By planning ahead, considering individual needs, and keeping an open mind, you can create a truly magical and enjoyable trip for your entire family.

Suggestions for child-friendly attractions, shows, and activities

When visiting Disneyland Paris with children, there are numerous child-friendly attractions, shows, and activities that cater to their interests and ensure an enchanting experience. Here are some suggestions to make the most of your time at the park:

Attractions:

- "its a small world": This classic boat ride takes children on a gentle journey through different cultures and showcases iconic Disney characters.
- Peter Pans Flight: Embark on a magical flying ship and follow Peter Pan to Neverland, experiencing breathtaking scenes from the beloved story.
- Pirates of the Caribbean: Join Captain Jack Sparrow and set sail on a swashbuckling

adventure through a pirate-infested Caribbean island.

- Dumbo the Flying Elephant: Children can soar high in the air on Dumbos back as they control their own flying elephant.
- Mad Hatters Tea Cups: Spin and twirl in oversized teacups inspired by Alice in Wonderland in this whimsical ride.
- Buzz Lightyear Laser Blast: Board a space cruiser and help Buzz Lightyear defeat the Evil Emperor Zurg using laser guns in an interactive shooting game.

Shows and Entertainment:

- Disney Princesses: Watch the Disney Princesses come to life in "Disney Princesses: A Royal Invitation" where little ones can meet their favourite princesses in person.
- Mickey and the Magician: Enjoy a captivating stage show where Mickey Mouse becomes a magician and brings Disney stories to life with awe-inspiring illusions.
- The Lion King: Rhythms of the Pride Lands: Experience a vibrant musical extravaganza inspired by Disneys "The Lion

King," featuring live singers, dancers, and acrobats.

- Disney Illuminations: A nighttime spectacular that combines fireworks, projections, and music to bring Disney stories to life on Sleeping Beauty Castle.

Activities and Interactions:

- Meet and Greets: Take advantage of the various character meet-and-greet opportunities throughout the parks. Children can meet beloved characters like Mickey Mouse, Minnie

Mouse, and the Disney Princesses.

- Autopia: Let your little ones get behind the wheel and drive their own miniature car on a scenic track.
- Alices Curious Labyrinth: Explore the whimsical maze inspired by Disneys "Alice in Wonderland" and encounter iconic characters from the story.
- Ratatouille: The Adventure: Shrink down to the size of a rat and go on a 4D adventure through Gusteaus restaurant in this immersive attraction.

Parades and Cavalcades:

- Disney Stars on Parade: Watch a vibrant procession of beloved Disney characters as they dance and march through the park.
- Disneys Once Upon a Dream Parade: Join Disney Princesses, classic characters, and colourful floats in this enchanting parade.
- Character Cavalcades: Keep an eye out for spontaneous mini-parades throughout the day, featuring favourite characters like Mickey, Minnie, and more.
- Remember to check the daily schedule for showtimes and

parades to plan your day accordingly. Additionally, Disneyland Paris offers seasonal events and special experiences throughout the year, so be sure to look out for any temporary attractions or shows that may enhance your visit.

Tips on maintaining a comfortable and enjoyable experience for the whole family

Maintaining a comfortable and enjoyable experience for the whole family during your visit to Disneyland Paris requires some planning and consideration. Here are some tips to ensure everyone has a fantastic time:

Dress comfortably: Wear lightweight and breathable clothing, especially during warmer months, to stay comfortable throughout the day. Consider bringing extra layers for cooler evenings. Comfortable footwear is essential since youll be doing a lot of walking.

Stay hydrated and nourished: Bring refillable water bottles and take advantage of water fountains and free cups of water available at food locations to stay hydrated. Pack snacks to keep energy levels up between meals. Disneyland Paris also offers a variety of dining options to suit different tastes and dietary needs.

Plan for breaks: Pace yourselves and take breaks throughout the day. Find shaded areas, rest spots, or indoor attractions to rest, cool down, and recharge. This is especially important for young children and older family members who may tire more easily.

Utilise FastPass and single rider options: Take advantage of the FastPass system to reduce wait times for popular attractions. Single rider lines are also available for certain rides, allowing members of your family to experience the attraction separately but with shorter wait times.

Make use of baby care centres: Disneyland Paris has baby care centres equipped with changing tables, nursing rooms, and feeding areas. Utilise these facilities to tend to the needs of infants and toddlers.

Create a flexible itinerary: While its good to have a general plan, allow for flexibility and be open to spontaneous experiences. This will give you the freedom to explore attractions that catch your interest and adjust plans based on the preferences and energy levels of your family members.

Take advantage of Extra Magic Hours: If youre staying at a

Disneyland Paris hotel, make use of Extra Magic Hours, where you can access certain areas of the park before it opens to the general public. This can be a great way to experience popular attractions with shorter queues.

Use Rider Switch for height-restricted attractions: If you have young children who do not meet the height requirements for certain rides, take advantage of the Rider Switch program. This allows one adult to wait with the child while the other adults ride the attraction. Then, the waiting adult can switch places without waiting in line again.

Stay connected: Set a meeting point in case anyone gets separated during the day. Ensure everyone has a means of communication, whether its through mobile phones or walkie-talkies, to stay in touch and regroup if needed.

Capture the memories: Take photos and videos to capture the magical moments throughout the day. Consider using Disneys PhotoPass service or assigning a family member as the designated photographer to ensure everyone gets to be in the pictures.

Enjoy nighttime entertainment: Dont miss the spectacular nighttime shows and fireworks. Find a good viewing spot early to secure a great view for the whole family.

Remember, the key to maintaining a comfortable and enjoyable experience is to be mindful of everyones needs, stay flexible, and communicate with each other. By implementing these tips, you can create lasting memories and ensure a fantastic time for the whole family at Disneyland Paris.

Chapter 7: Beyond the Parks

Recommendations for exploring the surrounding area of Disneyland Paris

Exploring the surrounding area of Disneyland Paris offers a wealth of opportunities for visitors to enhance their trip and make the most of their time in the region. From historic landmarks to picturesque towns and beautiful countryside, there are plenty of attractions and activities to discover beyond the enchantment of the theme park itself. Here are some recommendations for exploring the surrounding area of Disneyland Paris:

Visit the Palace of Versailles: Located just a short distance from Disneyland Paris, the Palace of Versailles is an iconic UNESCO World Heritage site and a must-visit destination. Explore the opulent halls, lavish gardens, and stunning architecture of this grand palace, which was once the residence of French kings and queens.

Explore the town of Meaux: Situated approximately 25 kilometres east of Disneyland Paris, Meaux is a charming town with a rich cultural heritage. Dont miss the magnificent Meaux Cathedral, stroll along the picturesque banks of the Marne River, and indulge in some delicious Brie de Meaux cheese, which is a local specialty.

Discover the mediaeval charm of Provins: A little over an hours drive from Disneyland Paris, the town of Provins transports visitors back in time with its well-preserved mediaeval architecture and fascinating history. Explore the fortified walls, visit the impressive Provins Cathedral, and witness thrilling mediaeval shows and reenactments.

Experience the magic of Château de Fontainebleau: Located approximately 50 kilometres southeast of Disneyland Paris, the Château de Fontainebleau is another exquisite royal residence worth exploring. Wander through its beautifully furnished rooms, admire the stunning gardens, and learn about the châteaus rich history, which spans over eight centuries.

Take a day trip to Paris: With Disneyland Paris being just a short distance away, a visit to the French capital is highly recommended. Discover iconic landmarks such as the Eiffel Tower, Louvre Museum, Notre-Dame Cathedral, and Champs-

Élysées. Enjoy a leisurely stroll along the Seine River, savour delectable French cuisine, and immerse yourself in the vibrant atmosphere of this global city.

Enjoy the tranquillity of the French countryside: Surrounding Disneyland Paris are picturesque rural areas characterised by charming villages, vineyards, and rolling landscapes. Consider taking a leisurely drive or bike ride through the countryside, stopping at quaint towns like Chantilly or Senlis, or simply enjoying a peaceful picnic amidst the natural beauty.

Indulge in culinary delights: France is renowned for its exquisite cuisine, and the region surrounding Disneyland Paris offers a plethora of gastronomic experiences. Treat yourself to traditional French dishes at local restaurants, sample delectable pastries and desserts from local bakeries, and explore the diverse flavours of the region, including the famous wines from nearby vineyards.

Discover the charm of Montmartre: Located in the heart of Paris, the neighbourhood of Montmartre offers a unique and bohemian atmosphere. Wander through its winding streets, visit the iconic Sacré-Cœur Basilica, and enjoy the vibrant ambiance of artists, street performers, and quaint cafes.

Visit the Champagne region: Located just a short distance east of Disneyland Paris, the Champagne region is renowned for its world-class sparkling wines. Take a guided tour of prestigious Champagne houses, explore the vineyards, and indulge in tastings to learn about the process of Champagne production.

Relax at the Val dEurope Shopping Center: Situated next to Disneyland Paris, the Val dEurope Shopping Center is a paradise for shopaholics. Browse through a wide range of international brands, enjoy delicious meals at its many restaurants, and even find great deals on Disney merchandise.

Excursions to nearby attractions, such as Versailles or the Val dEurope Shopping Center

Exploring nearby attractions and going on excursions from Disneyland Paris is a fantastic way to broaden your vacation experience and discover the treasures of the surrounding region. From enchanting castles to picturesque villages and natural wonders, there are numerous destinations worth visiting. Here are some exciting excursions you can embark on from Disneyland Paris:

Château de Chantilly: Located approximately 40 kilometres north of Disneyland Paris, the Château de Chantilly is a magnificent Renaissance castle surrounded by vast gardens and a charming town. Marvel at the opulent interiors, admire the extensive art collection at the Musée Condé, and explore the stunning French-style gardens. Dont forget to indulge in the famous Chantilly cream, a local delicacy.

La Vallée Village: Just a stones throw away from Disneyland Paris, La Vallée Village is a luxury shopping destination that offers a wide range of high-end fashion, accessories, and homeware brands. Enjoy a leisurely day of shopping, take advantage of the tax-free shopping opportunities, and treat yourself to designer goods at discounted prices.

Parc des Félins: Animal lovers should consider a visit to Parc des Félins, a wildlife park located approximately 20 kilometres southeast of Disneyland Paris. This spacious park is home to over 25 species of wild cats, including lions, tigers, cheetahs, and leopards. Enjoy a guided tour, observe the magnificent felines in their natural habitats, and learn about the conservation efforts undertaken by the park.

Chartres Cathedral: Situated about an hours drive southwest of Disneyland Paris, Chartres Cathedral is a masterpiece of Gothic architecture and a UNESCO World Heritage site. Explore the intricate stained glass windows, climb the towers for panoramic views, and immerse yourself in the spiritual ambiance of this iconic cathedral.

The Loire Valley: For a truly enchanting experience, consider a day trip to the Loire Valley, located a couple of hours drive southwest of Disneyland Paris. This region is known for its breathtaking châteaux, including Château de Chambord,

Château de Chenonceau, and Château de Villandry. Marvel at the architectural splendour, stroll through the magnificent gardens, and discover the rich history of these remarkable castles.

Parc Astérix: If youre looking for more theme park fun, Parc Astérix is a great choice. Located approximately 35 kilometres north of Disneyland Paris, this amusement park is based on the popular French comic series "Astérix and Obelix." Experience thrilling rides, live shows, and interactive attractions inspired by the adventures of these beloved characters.

Monets Garden in Giverny: Art enthusiasts will appreciate a visit to Monets Garden in Giverny, situated about an hours drive northwest of Disneyland Paris. Explore the vibrant flower beds, stroll across the iconic Japanese bridge, and immerse yourself in the serene landscapes that inspired renowned impressionist painter Claude Monet.

Normandy Beaches: History buffs may want to take a day trip to the historic Normandy Beaches, located a couple of hours drive northwest of Disneyland Paris. Pay tribute to the D-Day landings of World War II, visit museums and memorials, and gain a deeper understanding of this significant historical event.

The Champagne Route: Wine enthusiasts can embark on the Champagne Route, which takes you through the picturesque vineyards and charming villages of the Champagne region. Visit renowned Champagne houses, take cellar tours, and indulge in tastings of the regions finest bubbly.

The Palace of Compiegne: Situated approximately 90 kilometres northeast of Disneyland Paris, the Palace of Compiegne is a grand imperial residence with a rich history. Discover its beautiful architecture, explore the opulent interiors, and learn about its associations with Napoleon Bonaparte and other French rulers.

Information on additional activities and entertainment options outside of the parks

When visiting Disneyland Paris, there are plenty of additional activities and entertainment options available outside of the theme parks. Whether youre looking for relaxation, shopping, dining, or exploring nearby attractions, theres something for everyone to enjoy. Here are some popular options to consider:

Disney Village: Located just outside the Disneyland Paris parks, Disney Village is a lively entertainment district offering a variety of shops, restaurants, and entertainment venues. You can find themed merchandise, catch a movie at the Gaumont Cinema, enjoy live music at Billy Bobs Country Western Saloon, or have a meal at one of the many dining establishments.

Golf Disneyland: Golf enthusiasts can tee off at Golf Disneyland, an 18-hole golf course designed for all skill levels. The course offers beautiful surroundings and a challenging game, providing a pleasant break from the theme park excitement.

Val dEurope Shopping Center: Situated near Disneyland Paris, the Val dEurope Shopping Center is a large indoor mall that houses numerous shops, boutiques, and department stores. From fashion and accessories to home decor and electronics, you can find a wide range of products to suit your interests.

La Vallée Village: If youre a fan of luxury brands and designer shopping, make sure to visit La Vallée Village. This outdoor outlet shopping destination features over 110 boutiques offering discounted prices on famous fashion, beauty, and lifestyle brands.

Spa and Wellness: After a busy day at the parks, unwind and pamper yourself at one of the nearby spas. Many hotels in the Disneyland Paris area offer spa facilities where you can enjoy massages, facials, saunas, and other rejuvenating treatments.

Horseback Riding: Explore the picturesque French countryside on horseback with various equestrian centres located near Disneyland Paris. Whether youre an experienced rider or a beginner, you can enjoy guided trail rides through forests and beautiful landscapes.

Sealife Paris Val dEurope: If youre interested in marine life, visit Sealife Paris Val dEurope. This aquarium is home to over 5,000 sea creatures, including sharks, turtles, and colourful fish. Its a great option for families and those looking for educational entertainment.

Château de Versailles: Located just a short distance from Disneyland Paris, the magnificent Château de Versailles is a must-visit attraction. Explore the opulent palace, stroll through the meticulously manicured gardens, and immerse yourself in the grandeur of French history.

Paris City Exploration: Take advantage of your proximity to the French capital and plan a day trip to Paris. From iconic landmarks like the Eiffel Tower and Louvre Museum to charming neighbourhoods like Montmartre and the Latin Quarter, Paris offers endless attractions, museums, shopping, and dining experiences.

Local Dining Experiences: Dont miss the opportunity to savour traditional French cuisine and explore local gastronomic delights. There are many restaurants and cafes in the surrounding areas that offer authentic French dishes, from gourmet

Michelin-starred establishments to charming bistros and patisseries.

Chapter 8: Disneyland Paris for Seasonal Events

A guide to the various seasonal events and celebrations that take place in Disneyland Paris

Disneyland Paris is known for its magical experiences throughout the year, but what truly sets it apart are the spectacular seasonal events and celebrations that take place. From enchanting festivals to themed parades and dazzling fireworks, each season brings a unique and unforgettable experience for visitors of all ages.

Spring:

- The Spring season at Disneyland Paris is marked by the famous "Swing into Spring" event, which usually takes place from March to June.
- Main Street, U.S.A. is adorned with vibrant decorations, colourful flowers, and topiaries that celebrate the arrival of spring.
- The park features special shows, parades, and

performances with Disney characters in their spring attire.

- Guests can participate in interactive activities, such as the "Goofys Garden Party" or the "Minnies Little Spring Train," where they can dance and interact with Disney characters.
- The Spring event also includes unique dining experiences, themed merchandise, and photo opportunities with stunning backdrops.

Summer:

- Summer brings an explosion of fun and excitement to Disneyland Paris.
- One of the highlights is the "Frozen Summer Fun" event, inspired by the beloved Disney movie "Frozen."
- Guests can immerse themselves in the world of Arendelle through shows, sing-alongs, and even the chance to meet Elsa, Anna, and Olaf.
- The park features lively parades, water-themed attractions, and special nighttime shows, such as the mesmerising "Disney

Illuminations" fireworks display.

- Guests can also enjoy water-based activities, including the "Moteurs... Action! Stunt Show Spectacular" and the thrilling "Big Thunder Mountain" water coaster.
- Summer also brings extended park hours, allowing visitors to make the most of their day in the park.

Halloween:

- Halloween at Disneyland Paris is a spooktacular celebration that typically takes place from late September to early November.

- The park transforms into a hauntingly delightful experience with pumpkins, eerie decorations, and a festive atmosphere.
- Guests can enjoy special shows, parades, and meet-and-greets with Disney villains in their Halloween costumes.
- The highlight of the Halloween season is the "Disneys Halloween Party," an exclusive after-hours event featuring unique entertainment, a parade of ghosts, and a spectacular fireworks display.

- Children can participate in trick-or-treating, costume contests, and interactive experiences like the "Goofys Skeletons Street Party."

Christmas:

- Disneyland Paris truly shines during the Christmas season, which typically runs from November to early January.
- The park is adorned with dazzling lights, shimmering ornaments, and beautifully decorated Christmas trees.
- Guests can experience the enchantment of a white

Christmas with snowfall on Main Street, U.S.A.

- Special holiday-themed shows, parades, and musical performances take place throughout the park.
- The "Disneys Christmas Parade" showcases beloved Disney characters in their festive outfits.
- The evening is filled with the magical "Disney Dreams! Christmas" show, a breathtaking projection and fireworks spectacle.
- Meet Santa Claus, enjoy ice skating, and indulge in traditional holiday treats at the Christmas market.

Insight into special shows, parades, and decorations during holidays and festivals

The park goes all out with special shows, parades, and decorations, creating a truly unforgettable experience for visitors. Whether its Christmas, Halloween, or any other festive occasion, Disneyland Paris offers a range of delightful experiences that bring joy to guests of all ages.

Christmas Celebrations:
During the Christmas season, Disneyland Paris transforms into a winter wonderland filled with twinkling lights, snow-covered

landscapes, and heartwarming holiday cheer. The decorations are nothing short of breathtaking, with Main Street, U.S.A. adorned in garlands, wreaths, and towering Christmas trees. Sleeping Beauty Castle becomes the centrepiece of the park, embellished with thousands of twinkling lights and snowflake projections.

One of the most beloved traditions is the Disneys Christmas Parade, featuring Mickey, Minnie, and their friends dressed in festive attire, accompanied by enchanting floats and lively music. Spectators can also witness the magical tree lighting ceremony, where the lights of the giant tree on Town Square come to life in a dazzling spectacle.

At nightfall, the park presents Disney Dreams! of Christmas, a mesmerising nighttime spectacular where projections, fireworks, and music intertwine to create an immersive storytelling experience that celebrates the magic of Christmas.

Halloween Festivities:
Halloween in Disneyland Paris is a spooktacular affair. From mid-September to early November, the park undergoes a transformation into a realm of eerie enchantment. The decorations take on a hauntingly delightful tone, with pumpkins,

ghosts, and other Halloween-themed ornaments adorning every corner of the park.

During this time, guests can enjoy the Mickeys Halloween Celebration Parade, featuring beloved Disney characters in their Halloween costumes, as well as spooky floats and lively dance routines. The Disney Villains also take centre stage in their own show, "Its Good to be Bad with the Disney Villains," where guests can encounter Maleficent, the Queen of Hearts, and other iconic villains.

The highlight of the Halloween season is the "Mickeys Halloween Party" event, an exclusive after-hours party where guests can dress up in costumes and enjoy trick-or-treating, special character encounters, and a unique Halloween atmosphere.

Other Seasonal Festivals:
Apart from Christmas and Halloween, Disneyland Paris hosts various other seasonal festivals throughout the year. These include the Spring Festival, celebrating the arrival of spring with vibrant floral displays, Easter-themed activities, and a colourful parade. The park also celebrates the Festival of Pirates and Princesses, where guests can join either the pirate or princess side and participate in interactive experiences and parades. Additionally, Disneyland Paris showcases the Swing into Spring

4>>>

44>

event, where beautiful gardens, topiaries, and seasonal decorations create a delightful ambiance. Guests can enjoy live music, street entertainment, and character meet-and-greets amidst the stunning springtime scenery.

Other Special Shows and Parades: In addition to the holiday and festival-themed events, Disneyland Paris offers a variety of shows and parades that run throughout the year. The daily parade, Disney Stars on Parade, is a colourful procession featuring beloved Disney characters and floats. The show is a true spectacle, with catchy music, vibrant costumes, and larger-than-life props.

Another must-see is Mickey and the Magician, a live stage show featuring Mickey Mouse as a budding magician who takes the audience on a journey through beloved Disney tales. The show combines impressive illusions, breathtaking choreography, and classic Disney songs to create an enchanting experience.

Moreover, Disneyland Paris often introduces new shows and parades to celebrate the release of new Disney films or commemorate special milestones. These limited-time experiences provide an extra layer of excitement and novelty for park visitors.

Conclusion

In the final pages of "DISNEYLAND PARIS: Discover the Enchantment of Disneyland Paris," as the sun sets on the breathtaking Sleeping Beauty Castle, a sense of wonder fills the air, mingling with the laughter and joy of families and friends. The magical journey through this extraordinary realm of enchantment has left an indelible mark on the hearts of all who have experienced its captivating allure.

As we reflect on the unforgettable moments spent wandering through the whimsical lands, from the bustling Main Street, U.S.A. to the far reaches of Adventureland, Fantasyland, Frontierland, and Discoveryland, it becomes clear that Disneyland Paris is more than just a theme park. It is a symphony of dreams where cherished memories are born, and where imagination dances with reality.

Within these pages, we have ventured into a world where beloved Disney characters come to life, and where enchanting tales unfold before our very eyes. We have marvelled at the intricate details that breathe life into every corner, from the immersive attractions to the meticulously designed landscapes. We have tasted the delectable flavours of unique culinary experiences, and felt the thrill of daring adventures that ignite the spirit of adventure within us all.

But beyond the tangible delights lies something even more profound—a profound sense of magic that transcends age and time. It is a place where dreams find a home and where the spirit of Walt Disneys vision continues to thrive, inspiring generations to believe in the power of imagination and to embrace the childlike wonder within.

Disneyland Paris is not just a destination—it is an invitation to believe, to dream, and to connect with the essence of joy. It is a place where fantasies are woven into reality, and where the extraordinary becomes the norm. It is a testament to the enduring legacy of Walt Disney, a testament that reminds us that within every heart lies a spark of imagination waiting to be ignited.

So, as we bid farewell to the enchanting world of Disneyland Paris, let us carry the magic within us, forever treasuring the moments that have made us laugh, cry, and believe. Let us continue to be inspired by the stories and characters that have touched our souls, knowing that the enchantment we have experienced will live on, guiding us through the challenges and joys of everyday life.

As the final pages turn, may the spirit of Disneyland Paris forever remind us that in a world where anything is possible, our dreams can take flight. And just as Walt Disney once said, "All our dreams can come true if we have the courage to pursue them."

Until we meet again, may the enchantment of Disneyland Paris forever light our way, igniting the fire of imagination and reminding us that the magic within us is infinite.

The end.

Dear Valued Reader,,

We hope this message finds you well and filled with the joy and magic of Disneyland Paris! We are reaching out to you today with a humble request that could greatly benefit the travel community and countless Disneyland enthusiasts around the world.

We would like to kindly ask for your support in reviewing and rating Ian Vaughans travel guide, titled "Disneyland Paris: Discover the Enchantment of Disneyland Paris." As fellow travellers and lovers of all things Disney, your honest feedback and opinions hold tremendous value and influence.

Why is your review so important? Let us explain.

First and foremost, your review will help potential visitors make informed decisions about their trip to Disneyland Paris. By sharing your experiences and insights, you will be guiding others in discovering the true enchantment that awaits them within the parks magical gates. Whether its sharing tips on the best attractions, hidden gems, or must-try dining options, your review will become an invaluable resource for those planning their Disneyland Paris adventure.

Moreover, your review will also serve as a vital feedback mechanism for the author, Ian Vaughan. Constructive criticism and positive affirmations alike will enable Ian to further refine and enhance the guide, ensuring future editions provide even more comprehensive and up-to-date information for fellow travellers. Your input will directly contribute to the continuous improvement of this travel guide, benefitting countless individuals for years to come.

In addition, your review carries weight not only within the Amazon community but also within the travel industry. Positive reviews can help boost the visibility and credibility of Ian Vaughans guide, attracting more readers and allowing the magic of Disneyland Paris to touch the lives of even more people. By taking a few moments to leave your rating, you are actively contributing to the dissemination of valuable knowledge and helping fellow travellers create lifelong memories.

We understand that life can get busy, and writing a review may not always be at the top of your to-do list. However, we kindly ask you to consider the impact your words can have. A few minutes of your time can make a world of difference in the travel experiences of others and ensure that Ian Vaughans guide continues to be a trusted companion for Disneyland Paris explorers.

Thank you from the bottom of our hearts for considering our plea. Your support means the world to us, and together, we can create a treasure trove of knowledge and inspiration for travellers around the globe. Let us unite in celebrating the magic of Disneyland Paris and help spread the enchantment far and wide.

With sincere gratitude,

Ian Vaughan

DISNEYLAND PARIS